NIGHT ANIMALS

Books by Daniel Cohen

NIGHT ANIMALS

VACCINATION AND YOU

ANIMALS OF THE CITY

SECRETS FROM ANCIENT GRAVES

THE AGE OF GIANT MAMMALS

CONQUERORS ON HORSEBACK

NIGHT ANIMALS

by Daniel Cohen

Illustrated by HARIS PETIE

JULIAN MESSNER **NEW YORK**

Published simultaneously in the United States and Canada by
Julian Messner, a division of Simon & Schuster, Inc.,
1 West 39 Street, New York, N.Y. 10018. All rights reserved.

Printed in the United States of America.
SBN 671-32258-3 Cloth Trade.
    671-32259-1 MCE.
Library of Congress Catalog Card No. 78-107064
Design: Marjorie Zaum K.

To my aunt
Florence Gibbons

Contents

NIGHT ANIMALS

1

The World
of Darkness

You are standing in almost total darkness. Strange and eerie noises fill the air. Some of the noises may be familiar to you—the hoot of an owl, the croak of a frog— but others you have never heard before.

In front of you is a tropical jungle. Slowly, as your eyes begin to get used to the dark, you can see the jungle better. Bats flutter through the trees. On one of the tree limbs a sloth, a curious creature that spends its life hanging upside down, moves slowly and carefully. Beneath the sloth, a large fat rodent called a paca noses its way through the underbrush to drink at a running stream.

It is hard to believe that you are not really in the jungle

Sloth

in the middle of the night. You are really in a zoo. The sounds are recordings playing through loudspeakers. The jungle is not real. It is only one of many scenes you can see in this very special part of the zoo.

By walking a few steps from the jungle, you find yourself looking into a cave. Fat toads and strange-looking lizards blink up at you from the cave floor. Bats hang by their feet from the roof of the cave. Occasionally one of the bats will begin to move and then take wing from its head-down posture. In the closed-in space of the cave, the bat flies with amazing accuracy. It never brushes against the stalactites which hang like icicles from the roof of the cave. It never bumps into the glass which forms one of the cave's "walls."

The cave and the trees and bushes in the jungle outside it are all artificial. They are made mostly of plastic. Even the stream is not real. It is operated by an unseen pump. The two displays have been copied from a cave and jungle on the tropical island of Trinidad. But this *is* a zoo, and all the animals are very real and very active.

The tropical cave and jungle are two of the exhibits in the World of Darkness, a new kind of animal house at the New York Zoological Park, or Bronx Zoo, in New York City. Instead of just putting an animal behind bars in a cage, the World of Darkness shows different kinds of animals in settings that look like their natural habitat. But what is more important, the World of Darkness shows noctural animals (animals who are active during the night hours) and crepuscular animals (animals who are active at twilight).

How often have you stepped up to a cage in a zoo and been disappointed to find that the animal inside was sound asleep? All you could see was a ball of fur in one corner of

The World of Darkness building at the Bronx Zoo in New York City.

the cage. The only movement was a gentle breathing. But later, long after you had gone home, and the zoo was closed to visitors, all the lights in the cage would be turned off. Then, that breathing ball of fur would suddenly spring into activity and begin prowling its cage.

People who work in zoos know that a sleeping animal is not very interesting or informative to look at. They also know that nocturnal animals sleep during the day while the zoo is open. How then could the zoo make the animal exhibits interesting? The answer was to try making the noctural animals believe that day was night. In this way, the animals would be active when visitors were at the zoo.

Through the years, zoos have tried various ways of fooling nocturnal animals. Sometimes they would keep a night animal's cage dark during the day, and light it up at night. This fooled some of the animals. But often the cage had to be kept so dark in the day that the visitors could hardly see anything. Also it was very hard to keep the cage evenly dark. There was always light coming in through the windows and doors, and the nocturnal animal would become confused.

Other zoos tried to take advantage of a peculiarity of night animals. Their eyes cannot see red light. Cages were illuminated with red light bright enough for the visitors to see the animals. This system worked for those animals who thought it was completely dark. But since it was hard to keep ordinary daylight out of the cages, not all the animals were fooled. Besides, some visitors found that the red light hurt their eyes, and so they could not see the animals very well.

The scientists at the Bronx Zoo picked the best ways of showing night animals. These are being put to use in the World of Darkness, the first zoo house in the world to be devoted entirely to animals who are active in the dark.

During the day, the enclosures in the World of Darkness are dimly lit or illuminated with red light. The animals inside think it is nighttime.

To make the animals go to sleep at night, they must be fooled into thinking that night is day. After the visitors have left the building, bright lights are turned on. The light makes the animals think it is day, so they go to sleep.

Since nothing like the World of Darkness had ever been built before, the scientists and zoo keepers who planned it had to face new problems. For example, they wished to build an exhibit that would show the flying squirrel in action.

The flying squirrel is a very common little animal of the American forests. But because it is very shy and active only at night, very few people have ever seen it.

In spite of its name, the flying squirrel does not really fly. It has a flap of skin which connects its front and back legs. The flying squirrel will climb onto a high tree branch and jump off. While in the air, it stretches out its legs and pulls the flap of skin between them tight. With this fold of skin spread out between its legs, the flying squirrel can glide, like a kite, through the air. It can glide from one branch to another fifteen feet away.

16

The World of Darkness people knew that zoo visitors wanted to see the little animal in action. So they planned an exhibit in which the squirrel would have to do a lot of gliding. They built a long narrow enclosure. High up at one end, they put the squirrels' den or home. High up at the other end, they put the dish containing the squirrels' food. Everyone thought that the flying squirrels would glide from one place to the other.

For some reason they refused to cooperate. They climbed down from their den, walked across the bottom of the cage to the other side, and climbed up to get their food.

The people at the World of Darkness had to figure out some way of keeping the squirrels from walking across the cage floor. They decided to add another animal to the flying squirrels' cage. What they wanted was an animal that could not climb up and hurt the squirrels' den or eat their food, but would stay on the ground to discourage the squirrels from walking. The animal picked for this job was the skunk. The skunk is also a nocturnal animal, and so it would be up and about at the same time as the flying squirrel.

The plan worked. Flying squirrels are timid and skunks are aggressive. The flying squirrels did not want to go walking around on the ground with the skunks. They were forced

to glide from one end of their cage to the other.

The World of Darkness and its exhibits are only a starting point. From them, zoo officials and scientists hope to learn a great deal more about nocturnal animals and how they can be shown to visitors during the daylight hours.

2

Who's Out There?

As THE SKY begins to darken, the night shift of the animal world takes over.

The songs and cries of the birds are the most familiar noises of the forest during the day. But at night most birds go to sleep. Only a few, like the owl and the whippoorwill, fly about in the dark.

There are many different sorts of owls, and each has its own particular cry. But there is only one sort of whippoorwill, and its cry is not like that of any other bird. It sounds just like a ghostly voice saying, "Whip poor Will."

Once you have heard that cry, you will never forget it.

Another noise you will hear is made by the frogs. Frogs are great nighttime noisemakers. The frog chorus changes according to the season of the year. In the early spring, you will hear the tiny spring peepers. These frogs are so small that they are easily able to hide in plants growing along the edges of ponds. If you do happen to see a spring peeper, you will find it hard to believe that such a small animal can make so much noise.

Later in the spring and summer, the larger frogs join

The little frogs called spring peepers inflate the air sacs under their chins in order to make a loud noise.

the chorus. Last of all comes the bullfrog, the bass singer of the frog world. The bullfrog is the largest and loudest frog in America.

Insects also make a lot of noise at night. In late summer and early autumn, it is the crickets that make the most noise at night.

But you cannot hear many of the night animals. Skunks, raccoons, opossums, and porcupines all come out at night, but make very little noise. They are shy and secretive animals, and they do not want anyone to know that they are around.

Even the deer prefer to look for food during the night hours. In the spring and summer, deer are most active when the sky is dark. Only in the winter, when the nights are bitterly cold and food is very scarce, are deer forced to go out in midday.

The change from day animals to night animals does not only take place in the forest, it happens all over the world.

Perhaps the change is most dramatic in the desert. During the day, the sun beats down and the temperature soars to 100 degrees and more. Most animals escape the heat by spending the daylight hours in burrows beneath the ground or inside caves. For this reason, during the day the desert seems almost empty of animal life. But at night, when the sun goes down and the temperature falls, a large number of animals come out of their burrows and caves.

The noisiest of the night animals of the desert is the coyote, whose mournful howl is well known. The oddest looking is the heavily armored armadillo. But there are other strange-looking creatures as well — for example, the kangaroo rat, a mouse-sized animal that jumps about like a kangaroo.

Some of the members of the desert's night shift are not very pleasant. The rattlesnake and the poisonous lizard called the gila monster usually hunt at night. Poisonous scorpions and the large hairy-legged spiders called tarantulas are also night rovers of the desert.

In the jungle, the change from day to night is not as dramatic as in the desert, for the temperature does not drop as sharply. But there are still plenty of jungle animals that come out only at night.

The primates — the group of animals that includes monkeys, apes, and man — are mostly jungle dwellers, and many primates are nocturnal. Perhaps the strangest-looking

23

primate of all is the tarsier, a little nocturnal animal from the Philippines. The tarsier's eyes are so huge that it looks as though it is almost all eyes.

Most varieties of wild pig, particularly those that live in or near jungles, are active at night. Naturally those animals that class pigs as their favorite food — this includes the jaguar of South America and the leopard of Asia and Africa — also have to be active at night.

Nocturnal animals of the desert, from left to right: Scorpion and tarantula (inset), armadillo, rattlesnake, gila monster, kangaroo rat, coyote.

But we do not have to go to the jungle, the desert, or even the forest to observe the shift from day animals to night animals. The very same thing happens right in the city.

Unfortunately, most of the night animals of the city are not the sort of animals we like. Cockroaches creep out of cracks and corners in which they have been hiding. Rats and mice that have spent the daylight hours in cellars and other dark places come out only at night.

In the city, the insect we are most likely to notice on a summer night is the mosquito. Perhaps we don't always see this delicately built little creature, but we often hear it buzzing, and we certainly feel it when it bites us.

We can mention only a tiny sample of the enormous number of night animals that live throughout the world. But even this sample is enough to show that nighttime is not a time of sleep and inactivity for all animals.

3

The Hours
of Night

BEFORE CONTINUING with animals that are active at night, we must first answer the question — What is night?

Night is those hours between the time the sun sinks behind the horizon and the time it rises again in the morning. While it is daylight in one half of the world, it is night in the other half.

What causes day and night? To answer this question, try to imagine that you are an astronaut looking at the earth from outer space. You can see the whole earth. Half of it is brightly lit, while the other half is dark. The brightly lit part is the side that is facing the sun. This is the day side of the earth. The night side is the dark part of the earth, the part

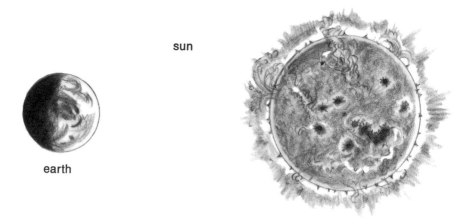

sun

earth

The side of the earth that is turned toward the sun is the light or day side. The side turned away from the sun is the dark or night side.

that is turned away from the sun.

The earth is not standing still in space. It is turning like a top. We say the earth is rotating. Every twenty-four hours, the earth turns completely around, so that everything is back where it started twenty-four hours before. The earth makes a complete rotation in twenty-four hours. During this complete rotation, all parts of the earth get both the hours of day and the hours of night.

From outer space you would be able to see that there is no sharp line between the light half of the earth and the dark half. They are really separated by a gray area. This gray area occurs because night does not begin suddenly.

You can find this out for yourself if you stand outside in the evening and watch the sun sink slowly behind the horizon. Even after the sun has completely disappeared from your view, the sky still stays light for almost an hour. This period is called twilight or dusk.

In the morning the process is reversed. Before the sun is visible above the horizon, the sky begins to get lighter. This period is called dawn.

Even in the middle of the night, the sky is not completely dark. On many days during the month, the moon shines very brightly. If you went out into the country on a bright moonlit night, you would be able to see fairly well, even at midnight.

When there is no moon in the sky, the light from the

stars still casts a faint glow on the earth's surface. This is known as starlight. Starlight is too dim to be of much use to human eyes. But to animals whose eyes are specially adapted for seeing in dim light, starlight can be extremely helpful.

4

Two Rhythms
of Life

THERE ARE more different kinds of land animals
active at night than are active during the daytime. The mammals — warm-blooded animals — are most likely to be up and
about at night. Reptiles, on the other hand, are usually
diurnal — that is, they are active during the daytime. Scientists say these are two different rhythms of life.

Why some animals are nocturnal and others diurnal
we do not know. Scientists have guessed that the two different rhythms of life began millions and millions of years ago.
At that time, giant reptiles called dinosaurs lived on earth.
Mammals also lived during the time of the dinosaurs. But
these mammals were tiny unimportant little creatures when

compared with the gigantic dinosaurs. The only way these little mammals could survive was by learning to hunt for food at night.

Mammals have an advantage over reptiles at night — mammals can keep warm while reptiles cannot. Nights are usually cooler than days, and mammals are able to be more active than reptiles in cool air.

Mammals maintain a constant or unchanging body temperature. That is what scientists mean when they say that a mammal is warm-blooded. We are mammals and our normal body temperature is around 98.6 degrees Fahrenheit. Our temperature remains about the same whether we are standing in the hot sun in the middle of the afternoon or in the chilly darkness of the evening.

The reptile's body temperature does not remain the same at all times. Its temperature is determined by the temperature of the air around it. When the weather gets cool, the reptile's body temperature falls, and it becomes slow-moving and sluggish. In order to become active again, a reptile must warm up. That is why we often see reptiles like lizards and turtles sunning themselves. If the weather becomes too cold, a reptile must hibernate or it will die.

Two Rhythms of Life

In the millions of years since the time of the dinosaurs, night animals have developed many adaptations for living successfully in the world after dark. In the following chapters, we will look at some of these special adaptations.

5

The Biological
Alarm Clock

IN THE STATE of New Mexico there are a group of large caves known as Carlsbad Caverns. Carlsbad Caverns serve as the home for millions upon millions of bats. During the day the bats sleep inside the caves. But at the same hour every evening, all the bats fly out to feed on night flying insects. Within twenty minutes the millions upon millions of bats have flown out of the caves.

How do the bats know what time to wake up and go searching for food? They were asleep deep inside the dark caves, and they could not see the sun go down. Yet they all got up at the same time, just as if an alarm clock had rung. In a sense an alarm clock had rung, but the clock was inside each of them. Bats and all other animals, including you and I, have what scientists call a biological clock.

For a bat, its biological clock is very important. Bats eat insects that fly at night. The bat has to work very hard to catch enough insects. It cannot afford to waste time by oversleeping.

The insects like moths and mosquitoes that make up

Millions of bats fly out of Carlsbad Caverns in New Mexico every evening.

the bats' food also have their own biological clocks. Some moths fly out at night in order to sip the nectar from certain flowers that give nectar only during the night hours.

Scientists have often tested the biological clocks of night animals. Among the animals used in the experiments were mice, for mice are nocturnal. They sleep during the day, and run about gathering food at night. In the laboratory, mice were kept in cages. Inside each cage was a wheel that the mice could run around in. The wheel was attached to a machine that recorded the number of times the mouse turned the wheel and at what time the running occurred.

At first, the mice were kept in a room in which the lights were kept on for twelve hours and then shut off for twelve hours. About one-half hour after the lights were shut off, the mice began running around in the wheel. Before the lights were turned back on, the mice stopped running and went to sleep. The mice showed the usual nocturnal activity pattern — they were active in the dark and slept when it was light.

After the mice were thoroughly used to having the lights on half the day and off half the day, the scientists changed the pattern. The lights were left off all the time. This did not make very much difference to the mice. The

When scientists attached a measuring device to the exercise wheel in a mouse's cage, they found that the mouse ran around at night, slept during the day, and began running around again the next night.

automatic recording device on the machines showed that they started running around in the wheel at the same time they had when the lights were turned on and off. They also went to sleep at the same time. Like the bats inside the cave, these mice in the laboratory did not get up or go to sleep just because of the light or darkness. They were controlled by something inside of them — their biological clocks.

Since biological clocks are so very important, scientists wanted to find out more about them. They wanted to know where in the animal's body the biological clock is located. And just exactly how does it tell an animal when to wake up and when to go to sleep? These questions are not easy to answer. But experiments with another nocturnal animal, the cockroach, have given scientists some further information about the biological clock.

We find cockroaches very unpleasant animals. But they are very tough, and for that reason they can be used in many different kinds of laboratory experiments. Dr. Janet E. Harker, an English scientist, wanted to find out where the biological clock of the cockroach was located and how it worked.

Dr. Harker knew that the cockroach's blood, and the blood of other animals as well, contains certain chemicals called hormones. Hormones are known to control many of the body's workings. Dr. Harker believed that hormones also controlled the biological clock.

In order to test her theory about hormones, Dr. Harker first needed some cockroaches that did not have properly working biological clocks. She raised a group of cockroaches in a room that was always lighted. Instead of getting up at night like normal nocturnal cockroaches, these roaches would run around at any time and sleep at any time.

Dr. Harker then joined one of the specially raised cockroaches to the back of an ordinary cockroach by means of a glass tube. The two roaches looked like Siamese twins. Blood

Dr. Harker's experimental cockroaches.

from one cockroach could flow through the tube into the body of the other cockroach. Dr. Harker then cut the legs off the nocturnal cockroach, so that only the cockroach without any day-night rhythm could run around. It carried the nocturnal cockroach on its back. But the special cockroach began behaving like a nocturnal cockroach. Dr. Harker concluded that something in the nocturnal cockroach's blood had transmitted the night-day rhythm to the special cockroach. That "something" she believed was hormones.

Hormones are manufactured by groups of special cells

called glands. Scientists had long known where the different glands in the cockroach's body are located. Dr. Harker found that when she removed a gland that was located in the cockroach's throat, the insect lost its day and night pattern. She had proved that the cockroach's biological clock was controlled by hormones manufactured by a gland in its throat.

Dr. Harker knew that when she raised cockroaches in a room that was always lighted, their biological clocks did not work. It was obvious to her that light and darkness did have some effect on the biological clock. So she decided to test just exactly how different periods of light and darkness affected the biological clock.

As a first step, Dr. Harker kept cockroaches in a room that was dark for twelve hours and light for twelve hours. These insects showed the usual nocturnal activity pattern — they ran around in the dark, and were quiet when the lights were on. But then Dr. Harker changed the schedule and shut the lights off eight hours earlier than usual, and turned them on eight hours earlier. At first the cockroaches did not seem to notice. They ran around and slept according to their old pattern, even though this meant running around in the light for eight hours, and sleeping in the dark for eight hours.

Day after day, as the lights were shut off eight hours

early and turned on eight hours early, the cockroaches finally changed their activity to match the new times of light and darkness and began running around only in the dark again. This proved that animals could reset their biological clocks, but they could not do so at once. It took time for them to get adjusted to the new schedule of light and dark.

The keepers in the World of Darkness at the Bronx Zoo have learned a great deal about biological clocks from the animals in that exhibit. It was not enough just to make day look like night and night look like day. The nocturnal animal's biological clock had to be reset as well.

When an animal is to be put on display in the World of Darkness, it is first taken into a special room called a conditioning room. Each day that the animal spends in the conditioning room the lights in its cage are turned on a little later each morning, and turned off a little later each night. Finally the lights are not turned on in the daytime at all, but only at night. In this way the animal's biological clock is slowly reset. It takes the average animal about three weeks to get used to its new pattern.

A night animal flown from Australia to the Bronx Zoo has an unusual advantage. When it is day in the United States, it is night in Australia, which is on the other side of the world from us. So when an Australian animal moves into the World of Darkness, where day and night are switched, it does not have to go into the conditioning room at all. As far as such an animal's biological clock is concerned, nothing has changed.

6

The Eyes
of Night

Many night animals have eyes that are specially constructed for seeing in very dim light. And there are many different kinds of eyes in the animal world.

The vertebrates, the animals with backbones — mammals, birds, reptiles, amphibians, and fish — have eyes that are constructed basically the same way. In many ways, the eye of an owl or a frog is the same as your eye. This kind of eye is shaped like a hollow ball with a hole in one end. This hole is called the pupil. At the inside of the back of the ball is a layer of cells called the retina. Light bounces off the

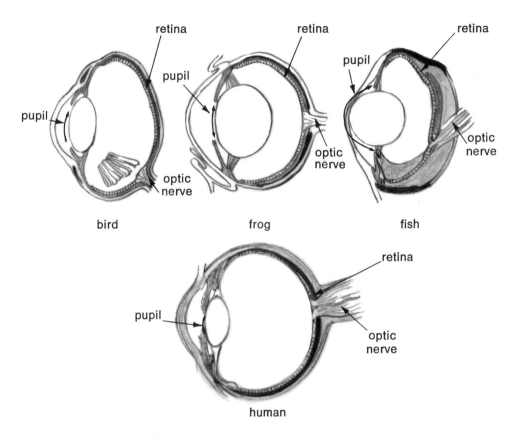

The eyes of vertebrates—animals with backbones—are basically similar in structure.

objects around the animal and enters the eye through the pupil. The light then hits the retina and is absorbed by it.

A large nerve called the optic nerve runs from the back

of the eye to the brain. When light hits the retina, it is changed into a nerve message. The message is carried by the optic nerve to the brain. The brain sorts out all the messages and builds them into the picture the animal sees.

Many night animals, including the owl, have very big eyes. The owl needs these big eyes so it can gather in as much of the faint light as possible.

Big eyes have disadvantages as well as advantages. You can look straight ahead, to the left, and to the right without moving your head. All you have to do is move your eyes. But the owl's eyes are so big that he has no room in his head to move them. An owl must stare straight ahead at all times. In order to look to the side, he has to turn his whole head. Fortunately for the owl, he has a neck that can easily bend in all directions. An owl can turn his head in almost a complete circle.

Size is not the only difference between the eyes of night animals and the eyes of day animals like ourselves. The retina of our eyes is made up of two different kinds of cells — the rod cells and the cone cells. They are so named because of their shape.

The cone cells are useful only when there is a lot of

light. They allow us to tell one color from another.

The rod cells are used when there is very little light. The rod cells in our eyes are what allow us to see objects on

The owl's eyes are so large that in order to look from side to side, it must move its whole head. For this reason, owls are able to turn their heads in almost a complete circle.

a dim moonlight night. But the rod cells do not give us the ability to tell one color from another. At night we may be able to see a cat walking across the lawn, but we will not

46

be able to tell what color the cat is.

Night animals need to see more in dim light than we do. Their eyes are packed with rod cells, but they have almost no cone cells. For that reason most night animals are color blind.

Here is the secret of why night animals are fooled by red lights in zoo buildings. When a red light hits the cone cells in our eyes, it causes the cells to send a message to our brain. The result is that this red light makes us see something. But the red light has no effect on our rod cells. The night animals who do not have cone cells in their eyes cannot see the red light at all.

Why does the red light have no effect on rod cells? Rod cells contain a material called rhodopsin. It is this material that allows the rod cells to pick up dim light. When we are in the dark, the rhodopsin builds up inside the rod cells. When exposed to bright light, rhodopsin is destroyed. It takes time for more rhodopsin to build up again. This is one of the reasons that it takes our eyes up to fifteen minutes to "get used" to the dark, after being in the light.

Rhodopsin is very good for picking up light in every area except one—red. This is because the rhodopsin itself is red in color. It absorbs all visible colors except red, which it reflects.

A night animal with only rod cells in its eyes cannot tell the difference between colors. But all the colors except red do have an effect on the rod cells. They cause the rod cells to send a message to the brain, and the color registers in the brain as a shade of gray. But since red is reflected out, it does not register at all. As far as the night animal is concerned, red light just does not exist.

The eyes of night animals have something else that our eyes do not have. Behind the retina of many night animals is a layer of cells called tapetum. These cells reflect light, just like a mirror does. In all animals some of the light that enters the eyes passes right through the retina without being absorbed by the cells of the retina. In daytime animals, this makes little difference. There is plenty of light to spare. But nighttime animals cannot afford to lose any light. That is where the tapetum comes in. Because of this mirrorlike backing, light that escapes the cells of the retina is reflected back. The cells of the retina then get a second chance to absorb it.

The tapetum is responsible for one of the most unusual characteristics of many animals — eyeshine. How often have you seen a cat's eyes "glowing" in the dark? The cat's eyes do not really glow — that is, they do not give off their own light. If the cat were standing in complete darkness, you would not be able to see its eyes. But if there is enough light shining into the cat's eyes, then some of this light will be

In bright sunlight, the pupil of a cat's eye is closed to a narrow slit. This slit opens wider and wider as the cat's surroundings become darker.

reflected back by the tapetum. This reflection makes the cat's eyes look like they are "glowing" or "shining."

Some night animals, like the cat, are also up and about during the day. Cats like to bask in the sunlight. But they must have special protection for their eyes.

When you see a cat's eyes "glowing" at night, they look wide and round. But in bright sunlight, the opening or

49

pupil of the cat's eye closes to a narrow slit to protect the sensitive cells from getting too much light at once. At night, this slit can open, like a pair of curtains, to allow as much light as possible to enter.

The pupils of our own eyes open or close, depending on the amount of light. When we step into a dark place from a lighted one, our pupils automatically open wider. The opposite happens when we go from a dark place to a lighted one. But the pupils of our eyes cannot open as widely, nor close as tightly, as those of a cat.

Night animals have eyes that are specially constructed for making use of very small amounts of light. But animals that live in complete darkness have no use for eyes. For example, some moles spend their lives digging underground tunnels, and there are fish that live in rivers deep inside caves. Underground or deep in caves there is no light at all. For that reason, many moles and cave fish are blind.

How well can night animals see in the faint light of night? The question is not easy to answer. The owl has about ten times as many rod cells packed into its eyes as a man does. With its specially adapted eyes, an owl can easily fly through a dark forest without hitting a branch or rock. A man walking through the same forest could hardly see anything. He would stumble and bump into things.

Scientific tests have shown that owls can pounce on a mouse in less than one hundredth of the light that it would take our eyes to see the same mouse. But scientists are not sure whether the owl depends only on its huge eyes to locate the mouse. Perhaps the sound or even the smell of the mouse helps the owl to find its prey.

7

"Seeing" with the Ears

NOT ALL night animals have large, specially adapted eyes like owls do. Many do not have eyes which are specially adapted for seeing in the dark at all. They rely on another sense — hearing — to find their way around.

Of all the night animals, those best fitted for getting around without using their eyes are the bats. There is an old saying about being "blind as a bat." Like most old sayings, this one is not true. Bats are not blind at all. Some bats, particularly the large fruit-eating bats of the tropics, have big well-developed eyes. They are able to see very well.

But most bats do not have particularly large or well-developed eyes. They can see well enough in daylight, but since they spend most of their time flying around in the dark, their eyes are of little use to them. Then how do they find their way around?

Most bats have big ears. These ears are the clue to their ability to navigate or find their way in the dark. Bats "hear" their way around. As the bat flies, it makes a series of noises. But we cannot hear these noises it makes; they are too high-pitched for our ears. For this reason, the bat's ability to get around in the dark remained a mystery for a long time.

When scientists began to experiment with bats, the first thing they did was test the bats' sight. They blindfolded bats and released them in a room. They found that the blindfolded bats could fly perfectly well. This proved that the bats did not use their eyes to navigate.

Next the scientists tested the bats' hearing. They stopped up bats' ears with cotton, but they did not interfere with their eyesight. These bats blundered into large objects which they should have been able to see.

Because of these experiments scientists suspected that bats used sound to navigate. But the scientists could not prove this because they could hear no sounds.

In the 1930s, Donald R. Griffin, who was a student at Harvard University, decided to try a new experiment with bats. He released bats in a room that contained special electronic equipment. This equipment could pick up the high-pitched sounds that our ears cannot hear.

As the bats flew around the room, Griffin could hear nothing. But a needle in a dial on the equipment was jump-

Scientists found that blindfolded bats could navigate perfectly well.

ing. This indicated that as they flew, the bats were making high-pitched noises. Griffin reasoned that the noises had something to do with the way bats navigate. The mystery of the bats' ability to fly in the dark had been solved.

This is how a bat navigates. The bat's high-pitched noise hits an object in its path and bounces or echoes off the object. The echo is picked up by the bat's large and very sensitive ears. By the sound of the echo, the flying bat is able to get a very good idea of the type of object in its path. The bat navigates by what is called echo-location.

How good is this system of echo-location for getting around? It is very good indeed. The bats of North America, and most other parts of the world, are insect eaters. By using their echo-location system, they are able to locate and catch tiny flying insects.

Moths are among the bats' favorite food. They have different ways of protecting themselves from hungry bats. Like the bats, many moths also have highly sensitive ears. These moths can hear the high-pitched noises a flying bat makes. When the moth hears a bat coming, it utters some high-pitched sounds of its own. These confuse the bat's echo-location system and cause it to lose track of the moth.

Some moths are covered with a soft powdery material.

This material absorbs the bat's sounds rather than echoing them back. In this way, these moths become "invisible" to the bat.

When some flying insects hear an approaching bat, they will simply fold their wings and drop to the ground, well out of the bat's range of hearing. Thus they avoid becoming a meal for the bat.

Bats drink as well as eat on the wing. A bat will swoop low over a pond or stream and take a sip of water in its mouth. A group of Central American bats are even more agile over the water. They have become fishermen.

Scientists are not entirely sure how these bats locate fish in the water. The fisherman bat has a long lower lip, and the scientists believe that this directs its sounds downward toward the water. When the sound bounces off a fish near the surface, the bat swoops down and catches it in its sharp, curved hind claws.

Another class of bats are called whispering bats. These bats make clicking sounds which are so faint that they can be detected only by the most sensitive microphones. Their echo-location system is not as good as that of the bats that emit high-pitched noises. It does not need to be. Whispering

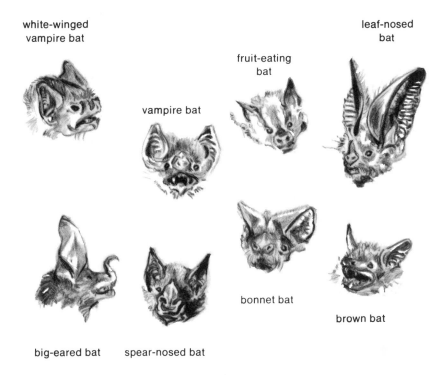

white-winged
vampire bat

leaf-nosed
bat

fruit-eating
bat

vampire bat

bonnet bat

brown bat

big-eared bat   spear-nosed bat

Because they navigate by sound, bats must have large ears.

bats do not catch insects in the air. Many of them are fruit eaters.

A whispering bat will hover in the air like a humming-bird or bumblebee. When it detects the echo from its whisper which has bounced off a piece of hanging fruit, it will land on the fruit and begin to eat.

Among the whispering bats is the famous vampire bat of South and Central America. This bat lives on the blood of birds and mammals, including man. The vampire bat hovers in the air until it locates a suitable victim with its clicking sound. If the victim is large, the bat will land nearby and crawl slowly and carefully toward it.

Vampire bats prefer to bite creatures who are asleep. But they do not suck blood. With their sharp teeth they nip at the skin, and then lap up the blood that oozes out from the wound. Their teeth are so sharp that they can make the bite without awakening the sleeper.

The bite of a vampire bat is not deadly. Men and large animals have been bitten many times without any bad effects. However, repeated attacks by vampire bats can bleed a small animal or bird to death. The great danger of the vampire bat is that its bite often carries disease, including the deadly disease of rabies.

A bat's method of finding its way around in the dark has often been compared to radar. With radar, airplanes can navigate at night and in storms when the pilot cannot see his surroundings. But this comparison is not quite accurate, since radar depends on radio waves. The word radar is short for *ra*(dio) *d*(etecting) *a*(nd) *r*(anging).

Submarines, however, use echoes of sound waves just as bats and other animals do. The use of sound waves in this way is called sonar, *so*(und) *na*(vigation) *r*(anging). Men have learned a great deal about sonar from the study of bats as well as whales and porpoises. These animals have small, weak eyes. Whales and porpoises continually utter a series of clicks and whistles. The echoes from these sounds give the animal more information about its surroundings than do its eyes.

Scientists suspect that other animals besides bats and whales use echo-location. Some small rodents make the same sort of high-pitched noises that bats do. They may use these noises for echo-location. But scientists have not yet tested these rodents enough to be sure.

Some night flying birds are known to have an echo-location system. The most remarkable of these is the oilbird of tropical America. Like the bat, the oilbird spends its days deep within a dark cave. When night comes, it gets ready to leave its nest in the cave in search of food.

While flying to the mouth of the cave, the oilbird makes a series of low clicking sounds. These echo off the cave walls and allow the bird to find its way accurately. But the echo-location of the oilbird is not nearly as well developed as that

59

The oilbird uses echo location to find its way
out of the cave in which it spends its days.

of the bat. Once outside the cave, the bird must rely on other means of finding its way around.

Since the oilbird is a fruit eater, it uses its sense of smell to find food. Only when it returns to its cave does it begin clicking again. The echo-location system of the oilbird is only good enough to detect and interpret sounds that echo from a solid cave wall.

8

Other
Night Senses

MICE WHICH ARE active mainly at night have good eyes. But they use other senses besides sight to help them find food and escape dangers in the dark. Perhaps sight is the sense they use least.

As the mouse moves through the night, it uses three other senses familiar to us: smell, hearing, and touch. Its nose is constantly twitching, on the alert to every odor. With its big ears the mouse can hear better than we can. Touch is also important to the mouse. Its long whiskers are extremely sensitive. If they brush up against anything unfamiliar, the mouse will immediately run away.

But the mouse has yet another sense which helps guide

it accurately in the dark. It is called the kinesthetic sense. The word *kinesthetic* comes from a Greek word which means movement.

What is the kinesthetic sense? Imagine yourself entering your bedroom after the lights have been turned off. In order to reach the light switch, you follow a routine you have followed many times before. You know that it is four steps from the door to the edge of your bed, then right turn and five steps to the wall, then left turn and five more steps ahead, raise your arm shoulder height, and there is the light switch.

The first few times you made that trip in the dark you fumbled around, first bumping into the bed, and then into the wall. But after you went through the same motions many times, you repeated them without thinking about them. In a way, you could say that your muscles "remembered" what the right path was.

We do not usually use our kinesthetic sense in moving around because we use our eyes. But a blind person can develop his kinesthetic sense to a very high degree. A blind person moving in familiar surroundings—his own room, for example—will move so quickly and surely that it is hard to imagine he is blind at all.

Even those of us who are not blind rely on our kinesthetic sense more than we know. A person who types "by
touch" is using his kinesthetic sense. A good typist does not
think about where the different keys on the typewriter are.
If he or she has to start thinking about the keys, he will begin
to make mistakes. A person who learns to play a piece of
music "by heart" is also relying on his kinesthetic sense.

Among animals of the night, the common house mouse
is a user of its kinesthetic sense. It is a real homebody and
does not like to wander. If undisturbed, it will not travel
more than a few hundred feet from the spot where it was
born. Night after night it will explore its tiny territory, relying on its kinesthetic sense — or "muscle memory" — to carry
it accurately through the darkness.

In addition to their echo-location system, bats also seem
to rely on a kinesthetic sense. To test this, scientists have
allowed bats to fly freely around a large room. After the bats
became familiar with the arrangement of the room, the scientists changed it. They put up a partition across part of the
room. Microphones in the room picked up the bats' high-
pitched squeaks, which indicated that their echo-location
systems were working. Still the bats blundered into the partition until they got used to it. The "muscle memory" of the

bats was so strong that they simply "couldn't believe their ears" about the new partition.

Most birds, even nocturnal birds like owls, rely on their excellent vision. But owls and other nocturnal birds also have exceptionally well-developed ears. A soaring owl can hear the squeak or rustle of a rodent that it cannot see.

Some nocturnal insect-eating birds, like the whippoor-will, the nightjar, and the frogmouth, do not have eyes that

Nocturnal birds from different parts of the world look strikingly alike. The frogmouth (left) is from Australia; the whippoorwill (center) is a North American bird; and the nightjar (right) is from Europe. All three have large mouths surrounded by whisker-like feathers. These "whiskers" help them feel insects that fly past in the dark.

are good enough to hunt for food. Nor are their ears well developed enough to do them much good. They seem to rely on touch and good luck.

These birds have very large mouths which are surrounded by whisker-like feathers. Moving along with their mouths wide open, they are able to gather in quite a large number of insects. If an insect escapes the bird's mouth, it may brush against the "whiskers." At the touch, the bird turns its head quickly and gobbles up the insect.

The bird most well adapted to living in the dark is the kiwi. This rare and strange bird lives only in New Zealand.

The kiwi has nostrils at the tip of its bill so it can smell worms underground.

It has been called the most nocturnal of all birds. Its eyes are so small that they are practically useless.

The kiwi has a long bill. While most birds have nostrils at the base of their bill nearest their head, the kiwi's nostrils are located at the tip of its bill. The kiwi thrusts its bill into the soft soil, and smells out burrowing earthworms, which are its main food.

Some snakes have very unusual ways of finding something to eat in the dark. They have special organs which allow them to detect heat. The pit viper is so named because it has two pits or holes, one on each side of its head. These pits contain their heat-detecting organs. The pit viper is so sensitive to changes in heat that it can tell the difference to a fraction of a degree. If the viper detects a warmer temperature, it knows there must be a warm-blooded animal nearby.

The Cuban boa makes constant use of its heat-detecting abilities. This snake's favorite food is bats. It hunts them while they are asleep in dark caves. It is too dark for the snake to see the bat, but it can feel the heat from the bat's body.

9

Night Lights

ONE OF THE most familiar sights on a summer night is the blinking lights of fireflies. There are many different kinds of fireflies, or "lightning bugs," in the world. Usually fireflies flash one by one. At night we see them blinking first here and then there. But in the jungles of southeast Asia, some of the fireflies have a more spectacular display. Thousands and thousands of them perched on leaves or branches will blink together, like the flashing sign of a theater sign.

Another creature that glows is the glowworm, which is not really a worm. It is the wingless female of a firefly known to scientists as *Phengodes*. Rather than lighting up its entire abdomen as most fireflies do, the female *Phengodes* glows with a row of bright points along its sides.

The firefly or lightning bug is also misnamed. It is not really a fly or a bug. It is a beetle of the family *Lampyridae*.

The firefly does not use its light to illuminate its surroundings as we would use a flashlight or lantern. Why, then, does it have a light at all? The firefly's winking light is a signal with which it hopes to locate a mate in the dark. The male firefly hovering in the air flashes his tail. When this

The firefly is a beetle whose abdomen glows in the dark. This flashing helps the firefly locate a mate.

female   male

signal is seen by a female, she flashes a proper response. The male follows this signal to come in for a landing near the female.

Each species of firefly has its own particular signal. Woe to the male firefly who mistakes the flash of the female of a different species. Fireflies are carnivorous — they will eat one another. The male that is not a possible mate may possibly be a meal.

The eggs of fireflies are laid on the ground, and sometimes these eggs glow softly. When the eggs hatch, the larva will spend a year or two eating, growing, and changing before it becomes an adult that is ready to mate. Some of these wormlike larvae glow. The glowing larvae may also be called glowworms.

Fireflies glow with a cold light. That is, unlike a light bulb, a fire, or the sun, the light of the firefly produces no heat. The light-producing organs of the firefly are on the underside of its abdomen. The familiar firefly glows with a yellowish light, but in tropical America some species glow red or green.

The light is produced by two products within the special cells. These products are called *luciferin* and *luciferase*.

Night Lights

Although scientists have studied the light of fireflies closely, they do not know exactly how it works. Can the firefly's light be harnessed by science for practical use?

Children will often collect a whole jarful of fireflies. But even when a mass of these creatures are glowing at their brightest, it is very difficult to read a newspaper by their light alone. A single firefly lighting up in the darkness looks very bright. But a jarful of them are very dim indeed when compared with a small light bulb.

The firefly is practically the only land creature that creates its own light. In the sea, however, there are a wide variety of animals that glow in the dark.

People who have sailed along coastal waters at night often see points of light flashing in the dark waves. These are created by a luminescent single-celled creature called *Noctiluca*. It glows when disturbed by the motion of the waves. There are many other tiny glowing creatures in the sea. Some enormous groups give the impression of a pool of light on the dark surface of the water.

But it is in the eternal night of the deep sea, down at a level below which sunlight never penetrates, that we find most of the world's luminescent animals. Here the majority

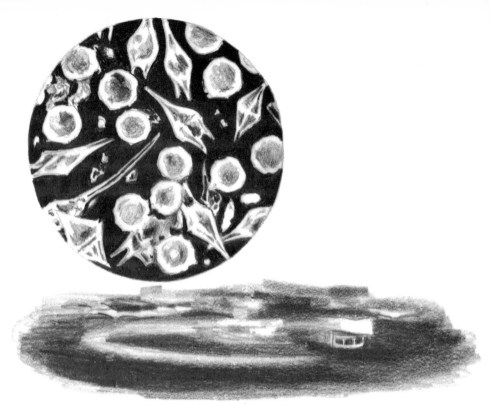

Many tiny sea creatures glow when they are disturbed, as by the motion of a passing ship.

of animals, be they fishes or squids or any of a number of shrimplike animals, have some sort of luminescent organs (organs that produce light).

The sunless depths of the ocean are a part of the world we know very little about. One of the things we do not know is how the deep-sea creatures use their lights.

However, we do know that all of them are carnivorous. The larger animals will eat the smaller ones. Yet none of them seems able to use its luminescence as a searchlight with which to hunt food. Although many of them have extremely well-developed eyes, their luminescent portions are so placed in their bodies as to be of little use in lighting up their surroundings.

Glowing spots on the side or the top of the head would seem to attract enemies rather than to be of any use in hunting food. But since most deep-sea creatures are luminescent, their light must serve some purpose. Perhaps today's increasing exploration of the depths of the ocean will help solve the mystery.

10

Wings
at Night

WE KNOW that most birds are active during the daytime. Many birds also migrate — that is, fly hundreds or even thousands of miles south to a warmer climate every fall and make the return journey northward every spring. Yet a large percentage of diurnal birds make their long migratory flights during the night and rest during the day. Scientists have long wondered why these birds reversed their normal activity pattern when migrating.

The mystery of night migration is only part of the much larger mystery of migration. How can a bird — like the indigo bunting, for example—find its way from Canada to Mexico and back every year? Sometimes the bird will return to the very same field it left the year before. But the birds have no map or compass to help them find the right direction.

In ancient times sailors did not have maps or compasses

either, yet they were able to find their way for long distances across the ocean. These sailors navigated by the stars. The pattern of stars in the sky remains the same night after night. The sailors knew that if they memorized the pattern of stars they could get a pretty good idea of where they were going. If the sailors wished to sail west, then they headed their ship toward a particular group of stars that they knew lay to the west. Was it possible, the scientists wondered, that the night-migrating birds also navigated by the stars just as the ancient sailors did?

In order to test the theory of migration by the stars, Dr. E. G. F. Sauer of Freiburg, Germany, raised warblers, a type of bird that migrates at night. In the fall, when the wild warblers were migrating to the south, Dr. Sauer noticed that his caged warblers became very restless and acted as if they too wanted to begin their migration.

Dr. Sauer then took his birds to the planetarium in the city of Bremen. He carried them in a covered cage. Inside the planetarium, an exact replica of the stars in the sky was projected onto a dome. The warblers were placed under the dome and the cover was taken off their cage. Immediately all the warblers in the cage faced to the south, the direction in which their wild relatives were already migrating. Somehow the birds had been able to tell direction.

Did the birds find the south by looking at the star pattern on the planetarium dome, or did they have some other means of finding direction?

In order to answer this question, Dr. Sauer covered his bird cage once again and had the star pattern in the planetarium shifted. This time the stars that should have been to the south were projected on the west side of the dome. When the cage was uncovered, all the warblers looked to the west.

When birds were placed under a replica of the night sky, they looked southward. That was the direction in which they would normally migrate. But when the replica was turned so that the stars which were usually in the south were put in the west, the birds looked to the west.

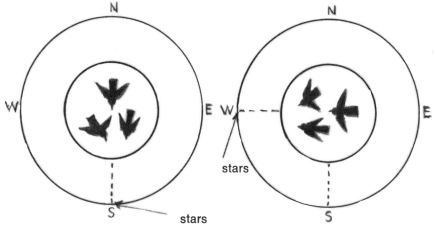

The birds got their sense of direction by looking at the stars. In the fall the warblers knew they were supposed to fly south. But the only way they could find out which direction was south was by looking at the stars. That is why they had to migrate at night.

Dr. Stephen E. Emlen, an American biologist, conducted similar tests with the indigo bunting. He took the birds to a planetarium and found that they hopped toward southern stars in the fall and toward northern stars in the spring. But he found that if all the lights in the planetarium were turned off, the birds simply hopped about at random.

Dr. Emlen's experiment helped to explain another puzzle about migration. Many birds refuse to migrate on cloudy nights. Other flocks of migratory birds seem to get lost and fly the wrong way when the sky is overcast. Scientists now know why. Without being able to see the stars, the birds have a hard time figuring out the direction in which they are supposed to be flying, and often they will simply fly at random.

Birds are not the only creatures to navigate by the stars. Moths also make use of starlight. But the moths do not look at the pattern of stars in the sky. The moth merely senses the direction from which the light rays strike its eyes. The moth adjusts its flight so that the starlight rays continue to reach its eyes at the same angle. As long as the angle remains the same, the moth will fly in a straight line.

When a moth tries to navigate by a nearby bright light like a streetlamp instead of the stars, its navigation system will no longer work properly. The moth tries to adjust its flight so that the angle of light from the lamp strikes its eyes the same way the starlight did. But this is impossible with the light from a lamp. So as a result, the moth makes a spiral flight toward the light. This is why you see so many moths clustered around a streetlamp or a lighted window on a summer night.

A moth's navigation system will become confused by a bright light, and the moth will fly a spiral path toward the light.

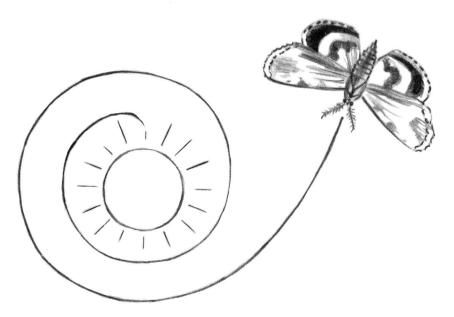

11

Lessons of
Night Animals

ONE VERY IMPORTANT way in which man is different from other animals is that animals adapt themselves to suit the conditions of the world, while man tries to change the world around him.

To find their way in the dark, night animals have specially adapted eyes, ears, and noses. They also use a lot of other senses. Because he is able to change conditions, man simply switches on a light so that he can see where he is going.

Long ago, primitive men were afraid of the dark and of the animals that lived in it. In their imagination these people filled the hours of darkness with all sorts of terrible creatures.

Most people today, particularly those who live in cities, have no such fears. Yet they do not really know what darkness is. Only rarely do people realize how much they depend on the electric light. On November 9, 1965, the northeastern part of the United States and parts of Canada suffered a tremendous failure of electric power. Almost all of the electric lights in New York, Boston, and Washington went off.

Very suddenly, people were faced with the darkness of night. The night of the power failure is called the Great Blackout, and no one who lived through it will ever forget it. People were afraid to move around. Most people simply sat in their homes or apartments for hours until the electric power was restored and the lights went on again. People realized that, unlike the night animals, their senses were not adapted to darkness.

But people who are used to getting around in the dark can do surprisingly well. Country folk, who often go out at night without the aid of artificial lights, learn to use their night vision. They give their eyes time to become accustomed to the dark, and are able to notice many things that escape the eyes of a person who is not used to the dark. Country people also depend heavily upon their hearing to tell what is going on around them in the dark.

A blind person lives in eternal darkness and must develop his other senses. A blind man's ears tell him a great deal more than a sighted person's do. A blind man's cane can be compared to the sensitive whiskers with which the mouse feels his way through the darkness.

By studying night animals, scientists are trying to develop new methods of helping the blind. There have been many experiments in electronics laboratories with sonar or echo-location. Devices that make faint noises have been tested. These noises echo from objects and are picked up through a set of earphones worn by a blind person. From the echoes, the blind person is able to determine what sort of object was in his path, in the same way a bat does. Scientists found that blind persons, when properly trained, were able to use an echo-location system with remarkable accuracy.

But such techniques as sonar for the blind are still in the experimental stage.

It is through research and the study of night animals that science helps to solve the mysteries of the world of darkness.

But most important, the more we learn about night animals, the more we will become aware of the wonder and importance of these wild creatures.

Glossary

AMPHIBIANS—Animals that must spend at least part of their life in the water.

BIOLOGICAL CLOCK—An animal's built-in ability to do certain things at certain times.

CONE CELLS—The cells in the eye that make color vision possible.

CREPUSCULAR ANIMALS—Animals that become active in the dim light of early evening.

DAWN—The time of dim light before the sun is above the horizon in the morning.

DIURNAL ANIMAL—An animal that is awake during the daylight hours.

DUSK—The time of dim light after the sun sinks below the horizon in the evening.

ECHO-LOCATION—See Sonar.

ETHOLOGY—The scientific study of animal behavior.

EYESHINE—The light reflected from the eyes of certain types of animals at night.

FIREFLY—A beetle of the family *Lampyridae*. Also called lightning bug and glowworm.

GLAND—A group of cells in the body of an animal whose function it is to produce a particular chemical substance called a hormone.

HIGH-FREQUENCY SOUND—Sound that is too high to be detected by the human ear.

HORMONE—A chemical substance produced by the glands that affects the functioning of the body.

KINESTHETIC SENSE—The ability to make certain commonly repeated movements without thinking about them.

LUCIFERIN AND LUCIFERASE—Two chemicals which combine to make a firefly glow.

MAMMALS—A class of animals that are usually covered with hair, bear their young alive, and have a constant body temperature.

MIGRATE—To go regularly from one region to another.

NAVIGATE—To find the way accurately from one place to another.

NOCTURNAL ANIMAL—An animal that is active at night.

OPTIC NERVE—The nerve that carries the sight impressions from the eye to the brain.

PLANETARIUM—A device that projects a representation of the stars in the sky.

PUPIL—The opening in the eye that allows the light to enter.

RADAR—A way of finding out the location of objects by using the echoes from radio waves—*ra*(dio) *d*(etecting) *a*(nd) *r*(anging).

REPTILES—A class of animals that usually have scales, lay eggs, and do not maintain a constant body temperature.

RETINA—The layer of cells at the back of the eye that absorb light.

86

RHODOPSIN—A substance in the rod cells of the eye that allows them to make use of dim light.

ROD CELLS—The cells in the eye that contain rhodopsin and are sensitive to dim light.

ROTATION—How the earth turns in space like a top. One rotation takes twenty-four hours.

SONAR—A way of detecting the location of objects by using the echoes from sound—*so*(und) *na*(vigation) *r*(anging).

TAPETUM—A layer of cells in the eye that reflect light.

Index

About the Author

DANIEL COHEN was born on March 12, 1936 in Chicago, Illinois, and received his education in Chicago public schools and the School of Journalism at the University of Illinois. Shortly after graduation, he started working for *Science Digest* magazine and was still working there as managing editor in 1968 when he decided to freelance as a writer.

In the field of science, Mr. Cohen has had numerous magazine articles published and is the author of six books. Married and the father of a daughter, Mr. Cohen and his family live in a farmhouse in the Catskill Mountain region of New York State.

About the Artist

HARIS PETIE, who was born in California, now makes her home in Tenafly, New Jersey. She attended art school in Rochester, New York, and Paris, France, where she lived for three years. She has illustrated children's books for most of the leading publishers.